PLAYING WITH GRAVITY

SOLI DEO GLORIA

PLAYING WITH GRAVITY

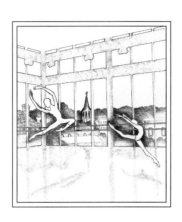

Poems & Translations

by

Joan Kunsch

joan Kunsch

For Manelich ~
Your depth of caring about
every movement in all detail
makes it a joy to watch you as
well as to work with you ...
Peace and Light ~
chocolate urge?
p. 100
Far North ~
final section
Norwegian hunters ~
p. 109
please see Notes ~
pp. 129 ~ 130

Joan

6/VI/'12

Antrim House

Simsbury, Connecticut

Printed in the United States of America
by Sheridan Books, Inc.

First edition, 2007

ISBN 13: 978-0-9770633-8-3
ISBN 10: 0-9770633-8-0

Library of Congress Control Number: 2007901169

Cover illustration by Joan Kunsch
Photograph of author by Howard Mortman, M.D.
Book Design by Rennie McQuilkin

Antrim House
www.AntrimHouseBooks.com
P.O. Box 111, Tariffville, CT 06081
860.217.0023

ACKNOWLEDGMENTS

Some of the poems in this volume were first published in the following periodicals, occasionally in earlier versions:

Atlanta Review: "Ballet Teacher's Brief Bio"
Two Lines: translation of "Misantropisk" ("Misanthropic") by Dag Sundby
Taj Mahal Review (India): "Psalm for a New Millennium"
Aftenposten (Norway): translation of "Sub Specie Aeternitatis" by Dag Sundby
Emmanuel: "A Question of Choreography"
Ibis Review: translations of "Sub Specie Aeternitatis" and "Søvnløs" ("Sleepless") by Dag Sundby
Ice-Floe: translations of "Et vindu mot Moldau" ("A Window on the Moldau") and "Transit" by Dag Sundby
The Researcher: "Elegy for Elderberry Aunts"
Twofer: "Koschka," "Remembering a Young Dancer"
Tzar-Katten (Norway): "Koschka," translated into Norwegian by Fernanda Sparre Smith
Voices Along the River: "Haiku"

"Ballet Teacher's Brief Bio" won an International Publication Prize in the 2006 *Atlanta Review* International Poetry Competition.

The section title "Rescued by Light" is derived from a line in the translation of Dag Sundby's poem "Søvnløs."

A quotation from *Brodsky: A Personal Memoir* by Ludmila Shtern appears courtesy of Baskerville Publishers, Inc.

An excerpt from "The First Elegy" of Rainer Maria Rilke's *Duino Elegies,* translated by Stephen Mitchell, appears by kind permission of Random House, Inc.

FOREWORD

Life as a teacher and choreographer in the world of classical ballet has added decades to the preparation time required for *Playing with Gravity*. Yet it is precisely the experience, contacts and collaborations along the way that have given this book its variety and scope.

My gratitude to my editor, Rennie McQuilkin, reaches beyond words. His towering understanding, surgical eye and encompassing knowledge of poetry have helped make this collection of poems the best it can be.

Encouragement and advice from many sources have benefitted this book. Among them are the Bread Loaf Writers' Conference and its Director, Michael Collier; the *Atlanta Review* and judges for its International Publication Competition; my sisters, Lisa Bosworth and Kathi Byam, and their husbands, Ray Bosworth and David Byam; Riva Berleant and Arnold Berleant, Michelle Childs and Starling Childs, Lois Lake Church, William R. Crochetiere, Sharon E. Dante, the late Dr. Frieda S. Flint, Eliza Gaynor Minden, Mary Gilman, Roger Greenwald, Dr. Ann Hutchinson Guest and Ivor Guest, Virginia Johnson, Lilly Kaplan, Holly Katz, Jorunn Kirkenær, Barbro Lillebø and Arild Lillebø, Barbara Marable, Carol Mock, Priscilla Newcomb, the late Juli Nunlist, Frank Oddo, Molly S. Oddo, Anbjørg Pauline Oldervik, Gloria Parker and Howard Platt, Anne Powell and Jim Powell, Elizabeth Sandia, Vladimir Shinov and Marina Porchkhidze, Ann Curtiss Scoville, Dorothy Skårdal, Fernanda Sparre Smith, Charlotte Story, Dag Sundby, Jane Tobler and Louise Willson.

Thanks and deepest appreciation to Momix, for a new vision and a new role; and to Connecticut's Nutmeg Ballet/Nutmeg Conservatory for the Arts, my artistic home.

Joan Kunsch
Torrington, Connecticut
December, 2006

PLAYING WITH GRAVITY

I   *this devious wand*

Ballet Teacher's Brief Bio	17
Back and Forth in Time	18
Advice to Myself	20
The Presence	21
Hibachi	22
Transit (Dag Sundby)	23
Transit (translation)	23
Å mine barn (Anbjørg Pauline Oldervik)	24
O My Children (translation)	25

II   *the fullness of empty space*

A Question of Choreography	29
Hall of Dreams	30
You Are Who Are	32
Technical Thaw	33
A Prose Poem to Momix	34
Figure-Ground	35
Ballet Studio with Glass Wall	36
Remembering a Young Dancer	37
Dancers Rehearsing	38
Pregnant Nude at Play	39
Berkshire Night	40

III   *rescued by light*

Night Beats	43
Breakaway I	44
Night Life	45
Et vindu mot Moldau (Dag Sundby)	46
A Window on the Moldau (translation)	47
Høysang (Dag Sundby)	48
Song of Songs (translation)	49

PLAYING WITH GRAVITY

Maktfordeling (Dag Sundby)   50
Power Trump (translation)   51
Sub Specie Aeternitatis (Dag Sundby)   52
Sub Specie Aeternitatis (translation)   53
Søvnløs (Dag Sundby)   54
Sleepless (translation)   55
Perle der inne (Anbjørg Pauline Oldervik)   56
Pearl in there (translation)   57
Mot et lys (Anbjørg Pauline Oldervik)   58
Toward a Light (translation)   59

IV   cobalt shadows

Elegy for Elderberry Aunts   63
Kathy Fiskus   64
Fever   66
Misantropisk (Dag Sundby)   67
Misanthropic (translation)   67
Solefall (Dag Sundby)   68
Sunset (translation)   68
Requiem for Richard Gilman   69
Silence   70
The Spiral Elevator Shaft   71
In January   72
O Most Mysterious   74
Fleeting Jewel   75
Louise and the Starshower   76
After the Picnic   77
Breakaway II   78
Psalm for a New Millennium   80

V   high clear notes

Koschka   83
Haiku   84

PLAYING WITH GRAVITY

Centipede   85
Mockingbird the Rapper   86
Dinner is Postponed   88
Open 24 Hours   89
"Freaking Awesome!"   90
Last of Summer   91
Offstage Choreography   92
Limerick   93
Manhattan Street Music   94
Mozart (Dag Sundby)   96
Mozart (translation)   97
Andrés Segovia   98
In Concert   99
Ode to Chocolate   100
For the Children of Zimbabwe   102
Connection Delayed   103

VI   *magnetic north*

White on White   107
Magnetic North   108
Into the Saga   109
By Northern Light   111
In Moscow   113
St. Petersburg: The Mariinsky   114
May Night   115
Encounter   117
Benjamin and Anna   119
Petersburg Pilgrimage   120
Sidewalk Saints   121
Between Rehearsals   123
Homecoming   126

notes & biographies   129

Writing has split open my soul.
To read these words
might make you my family.

I *this devious wand*

"Ideally, poetry is the negation of mass and the laws of
gravity by language."   –Joseph Brodsky

BALLET TEACHER'S BRIEF BIO

I teach flying
        have 2500 children
find eternity's height and breadth
        in small space
see my way by Northern Lights
        often arrive home
with foreign dust on my shoes
        thrive on leaves and seeds
am a bulldozer made of velvet
        listen for cello and church bells
meadowlark and mourning dove
        carry odd credentials
enter through the escape hatch
        define cobalt
by evergreen shadows cast on snow
        understand the mockingbird
declare the Russian Impressionists
        my godparents
and those with paw or wing, fur or fin
        my siblings....
I find much peace with tulips
        and Archangels

BACK AND FORTH IN TIME

for my cousin Elizabeth Sandia

Let us raise a toast
to our great-great forebear
who looked out over this eminence,
our family nose,
made merry with this
our clarion laugh — and tossed them
far down the line
to us. Did he leap barefoot
once upon a time
down cathedral aisles
fast often
to hear colors more acutely
write by sputtering café candles
wander a vast city all night
lean from its bridges
to watch the coming dawn
over a wide river…?
Did he make music?
Did he ever dream
forward in time
to our time
and awaken astonished
that we are female?

After us
let protégé,
painting, poem, ballet
— our only descendants —
spread the legacy of passion

for music, poetry,
dance, color;
may visions continue
of starry days
and suns at midnight,
yes, even the stubborn streak,
all the turmoil and technique,
light and laughter:
our legacy to be reborn
— all but the nose —
time after time.

ADVICE TO MYSELF

Danger ahead!
In my hand, this devious wand:
ballpoint
headed straight for a claptrap weekend,
a balderdash spree
of dead-earnest drivel.

Better to get outside,
jog the canal,
start fresh, asking nothing.
Then head back in,
wait, keep watch
as vigil edges toward vision.

Now begin:
Write.

THE PRESENCE

Writing prose
I'm on my own.
As for my poems,
someone else decides
when and where
they will come alive.
Who is it there
just out of sight
behind my shoulder?
Not Akhmatova's Muse
but perhaps her distant
cousin...My visitor
is not veiled
but may toss aside
a snow-wet scarf
and begin to hum
a Georgian lament
or a Scottish milking croon
before sounding from
throats of cellos.
The one who haunts me
is never twice the same,
always making me guess
from which threshold,
from behind which birch tree
or music stand
she will next appear...

HIBACHI

Trying to define poetry for the young
Chinese wait staff in a Japanese restaurant
I mention their great one, Li Po
and make scribbling motions on a napkin.
They shake their heads.
"Words that go to your heart,"
my friend tries.
They bring their Japanese boss
who does not recognize "Haiku."
Either it's going to take more than ESL
or I'm mispronouncing Li Po and Haiku
miserably. After learning the word
in both Japanese and Mandarin
I'll go back there, not to define
the undefinable, but just to say
"Poetry poetry poetry"
to each
in her native tongue.

TRANSIT

Vi skriver våre dikt
Som broer mellom stjernene i himmelrommet
Fra lys til lys i tomrommet
Mellom galaksenes *perpetuum mobile*
Vi tror det tvers igjennom
Neonlysenes iltre kamuflasje
Vi tror det ved kafebordet i solen
Og i de små sidekapellene
I tusmørket i de store katedralene
Vi tror på broene i mørket over oss
Fra galakse til galakse
Over til lyset som bor
I hver vår verden

Dag Sundby

TRANSIT

We write our poems
As bridges between stars in space
From one light to another in the void
Through the galaxies' *perpetuum mobile*
This we believe in straight through
The brash camouflage of neon lights
We believe it at outdoor cafés in the sun
And in small side chapels
Edging the semi-darkness of great cathedrals
We believe in bridges through the darkness over us
From galaxy to galaxy
Across to the light which abides
In each one's own inner world

J.K.

Å mine barn
ligger så stille i mitt bryst
grav ved grav
hjelp meg å gråte

Fly ut fra mine fingerspisser
kom opp kom opp fra hendenes reder
hvert hjerteslag fødsler
hver gang munnen åpner seg nye flyveferdige
fugl på fugl
ut med min ånde

Syngende piler rappe slag bløtt sus i luften
se de løses fra tå efter tå se som de svinger seg
ut fra min hæl
løfter seg flokkevis seiler over issen
leker og lander
hviler på vingen og daler stiger synker setter seg
i fred på min panne til morgenen

Anbjørg Pauline Oldervik

O my children
lying so still in my breast
grave by grave
help me to weep

Fly out from my fingertips
come up come up from the nests of my hands
each heartbeat gives birth
every time my mouth opens new fledglings
bird after bird
out with my breath

Singing arrows rapid strokes soft sigh in the air
see them set loose from toe after toe
see how they swing out of my heel
lift off in flocks sail over my crown
play and land
rest on the wing and descend rise sink settle down
in peace on my forehead until morning

J.K.

II   the fullness of empty space

A QUESTION OF CHOREOGRAPHY

Who dances into mind
when images appear
with bodies light enough
to be anywhere thought moves them?
Figures wreathe into slow falls
  play with gravity
     spin at any speed
       leap rainbow spans
     rise or plummet
   through endless diagonals.
Transparent, cleared of self,
they arrive as ideas, bearing
motion, shape, line, even color —
never personality.   At rehearsal
their movement translates into life
   for concert ballets
     sacred space
       films and festivals
     art gallery openings
   psalms for the feet:
Choreography! Motion from where?
Who is it dancing
when images come to mind?
Others may speak of a Muse. Look there —
an ethereal playground
for countless beings made of light.
All dancing.

HALL OF DREAMS

Act I

All of us kids sat
around twelve Sunday School tables
singing "Onward Christian Soldiers"
in the First Lutheran gym.
While my father
retold parables, I'd gaze up
at rows of Swan Maidens
who would ripple their arms
into feathered wings
when the Prince leaped onstage.
After choir practice on Friday nights
the space became a teenage dance floor.

I stood wallflower duty
on the girls' side, listening:
"Each night I ask
the stars up above
Why must I be-ee
a teenager in love..."
There were plenty of boys opposite
but the walk across was long
and I was not the cute one.
Meanwhile, just beyond
the swaying couples
and clearly visible
was the Firebird
soaring in scarlet,
bewitched by the evil Sorcerer,
dropping a golden feather
to dazzle the young Tsarevitch.

Stravinsky themes in my head
drowned out the crooner:
"To know-know-kno-oh him
is to love-love-luh-uhv him…"
A chaperone nudged the pimpled boy
who trudged over
and invited me to dance
the very last phrase
of the last song.

Act II

Decades later
comes an invitation
to stage a ballet
in the hall of my visions
—now transformed
into a ballet studio.
A glance beyond barres and mirrors
reverses the dream,
brings back my father
teaching Sunday School,
my reluctant partner,
the damp breathless girls
whirling with good Lutheran boys.
"Onward…" the hymn re-echoes.

Today
aspiring swans and firebirds
line up at the barre
waiting for me.
We begin with pliés.

YOU ARE WHO ARE

You, transparent
dance between flame and mirror
You utter the silence
between lightning bolt
and thunderclap
Inextinguishable
you gaze
into my soul
so I blaze:
liaison
between fledglings
and light

TECHNICAL THAW

It would have been good
to spend the day here
stranded, sipping tea,
abandoned to the spell of words.
("Cancellations? No, My'um,
we's a hah-tech airport!")
Later, a cubicle hovers
over our silver wing
emitting pink de-icer spray.
The huge, the white sky
leans close, as if
to snatch us up
toward the next city, where
young dancers await their audition.
My role: to find and free
the hidden wings
so they too
will be able to soar.

A PROSE POEM TO MOMIX

Surrounded by dancers, I teach class in a barn. Damp fabric clings to working muscle as each day's miracle is repeated: whether sore and cautious, drowsy or well-rested, breakfasted or not, each dancer enters the flow of company class. Limbs and torsos surge upward and sink, stretch and contract, bend and expand, attain full movement fluidity and control. Here and there a random sunray spotlights the sculpture of a clavicle, the defined curve of a calf muscle used to its limit.

Here one can feel music pulsate like a mother's womb as she prepares to give birth. Eighteen dancers labor and rejoice — Widen the floor, raise the roof, fill space with new work being born! Soon these movements will bring a sparkle back into the eyes of tired Dutch bankers; will cause Brazilian youths to leap from their plush theatre seats in a jumping ovation; will shift the French economy as whole audiences resolve to become lighter on their own feet by ignoring *le croissant*.

A secret is nurtured in the seclusion of Connecticut woods. Nothing anywhere seems remote, unreachable. To be at work here is to be completely in touch.

Momix is an international touring company led by Moses Pendleton, Artistic Director, and Cynthia Quinn, Associate Director, and based in Washington, Connecticut.

FIGURE-GROUND

Soon I'll invent a mantra of zero syllables,
a choreography for air currents
around motionless dancers.

BALLET STUDIO WITH GLASS WALL

for my students

You balance in arabesque
      behind you rises autumn mist
You are swept into story by one in a cape
      last leaves tremble in gusts of wind
Fingertips reach along infinite line
      wild geese course past clouds
A double cabriole clears the horizon
      below lie city rooftops
Pirouettes mimic leaves whirling free
      street lamps flicker on at dusk
Caught by a partner you rise and are gone
      hillsides blend with night sky
Empty space is alive where you have danced

REMEMBERING A YOUNG DANCER

You
little bell
shiver of laughter
skip
spring
sprinkle sunspace
with pigtails bobbing
blur of freckles
elf-daughter
mes(merry)merizing hardwood
into springing you aloft
conspiring with upper air
to keep you

From far forgotten corners
traces of rosin dust
are whipped into orbit
roused by magnetic passage
of pointes
polyrhythms
shivers of laughter
little bell
you

DANCERS REHEARSING

after the manner of Gertrude Stein

Here is one seeming more soaring.
She springs up and she casts into air
her whole body
and I can notice it I can notice
her staying in the air. Today we have
six together but only one above earth.
I mean by that to say four are interlacing,
crossing, bending and one more is lifting
one other. What is the current
that takes her up, that takes her above
other ones walking, working, weaving.
What is the current that drifts
along a long line then rises
into necesssary flight.
What is this current.
This upward current.
I aloft alongside.

PREGNANT NUDE AT PLAY

Handstand
in a rushing stream
water-flung reflections
brocade the skin
of belly and flank
Her unborn son
tries the new feeling
of head above heels
as he floats
within
her perfectly centered
equilibrium

BERKSHIRE NIGHT

Silvermoondisc rises
through black lace
branches over mountain pond.
Tree trunks, ferns and woman
lean out over water
on a night when nothing
is vertical.
Ripples
cradle and rock
a thousand moons.
Near and distant lamps
— jewels of a necklace —
encircle the shore.
The swaying dock
like a waltz partner
bobs and tilts the woman:
easy balance
backward bend
face to the stars

breathe light
taste wind

out there over water
with palms open
arms lifted

she can almost
touch her children's faces —

III   *rescued by light*

NIGHT BEATS

Two a.m., the clock says.
Thump the bed, find the cat.
Salad and a slice of meat
were not enough for dinner.
You, my companion rain,
are not drumming,
drumming enough
to drown out that other beat,
beat, that beat, that heart
that lay upon my own.

Last night, limbo. Oblivion.
It's second nights alone
that trudge sleepless
into cold dawns.

BREAKAWAY I

After all you poets have left us
of consolation, we still
haven't mastered partings.
Final hours tear through us.
Some cannot love without possessing
and some who love will not be
possessed.
We spangle the sky
with our gleaming jets,
our parting tears.

Dancer,
how well you know: spinning fast
dries tears.

NIGHT LIFE

Often in dreams I am waving farewell to you
through double glass panes: my taxi
or train window and yours,
somewhere in Russia. Last night
you were en route to your past
via the "Moskoview Express"
while I set out in the opposite direction
to be a guest choreographer somewhere.
Other nights the dream luggage evaporates
or we have to run faster than fire
or the address we urgently seek
proves to be non-existent
just as the boulevard of our destiny dwindles
into a gravel path along a fence.
Yet in each dream is a sense
of our having decoded the message
found the lost children
lived through the siege
glimpsed the splendor
— only to part
certain of reunion
at an understood
place and time
we never name.

ET VINDU MOT MOLDAU

I ettermiddag omtrent
Ved sekstiden da solen
Fra Moldau opp
Gjennom våre vinduer
Mot ditt venstre kinn
Slettet alle sorger ut av
Ditt ansikt elskede
Så jeg i denne skjønnhet
Alt det som skulle ha vært
Alt det jeg hadde villet
Med alt mitt strev
Og jeg trakk gardinet for

Dag Sundby

A WINDOW ON THE MOLDAU

Late this afternoon around
Six o'clock when the sun
From the Moldau
Up through our window
Onto your left cheek
Erased all cares from
Your face beloved
I saw in that beauty
All that should have been
All I had intended
With the sum of my toil
And I pulled the curtain closed

J.K.

HØYSANG

Du, min elskede
som var, er og alltid blir
Du, fra hvis navle verden
igjen får mening
Du, dine brysters
Hallelujah og din halsgrops
hemmelighet,
Du, dine hofters lys
i allskens mørke
Du, min elskede
min uvisnelige
Mine veier jevner du ut,
skyggefulle trær
lar du kranse dem,
øynene dine opplyser dem
Dine hender holder mitt hode
vendt mot lyset
for utenfor deg hersker natten
Du bare, er lys
og alle tings fortsettelse
Du, min daglige oppstandelse
skynd deg
skynd deg hjem med ditt beger
at jeg kan fylle det
så vi får drikke og leve
våre liv igjen
og igjen

Dag Sundby

SONG OF SONGS

You, my beloved
who were, are and ever shall be
You, from whose navel the world
once more takes on meaning
You, the Hallelujah of your breasts
and the secret hollow of your throat
You, your hips alight
however deep the darkness
You, my beloved
my imperishable
You make my paths level,
wreathing them
in shade trees,
your eyes illuminate them
Your hands hold my head
toward the light
for apart from you night reigns
Only you are light
and continuance of all things
You, my daily resurrection
hurry
hurry home with your cup
that I may fill it
and we'll drink and live
our lives over
and over again

J.K.

MAKTFORDELING

Stillferdig som en verdenskrig
går du gjennom rommene
Uovervinnelig knuser du meg
med dine smil
I betingelsesløs underkastelse
legger jeg meg tilrette
for dommens ubønnhørlighet

Mens du må holde din seier
vedlike, dyrke din makt
fyller jeg som slave frydefullt
hver dag din styrkes beger

Dag Sundby

POWER TRUMP

Gentle as a world war
you pass through the rooms
Unconquerable you crush me
with your smiles
In unconditional surrender
I submit
before implacable judgment

While you must hold onto your triumph
maintain and cultivate your power
I, your joyous slave, fill
every day the chalice of your strength

J.K.

SUB SPECIE AETERNITATIS

Varighet er et relativt begrep
sub specie aeternitatis
jeg husker for eksempel
fremdeles dine leppers bue
men har allerede glemt
fasongen på Mount Everest
enda jeg har fløyet over der
mange ganger

Og fjellet står ennå
mens du og dine lepper
forlengst er blitt jord

I en ny verden kanskje
møter jeg igjen ditt smil
lenge etter at Mount Everest
er blitt sand
på bunden av et hav

Dag Sundby

SUB SPECIE AETERNITATIS

Permanence is a relative concept
sub specie aeternitatis
I still remember for example
the curve of your lips
but have already forgotten
the shape of Mount Everest
though I have flown over it
many times

And the mountain is still standing
while you and your lips
have long since turned to earth

In a new world perhaps
I will meet your smile again
long after Mount Everest
has become sand
at the bottom of a sea

J.K.

SØVNLØS

Jovisst er jeg dødsens
redd himmelrommet og de brune
flekkene på hendene mine
De nattlige konserter
for hjerteslag og pauker
tuba og trommer
Allegro con fuoco
i stadig smalere spiraler
mot infarctets uavvendelige klimaks

Reddet av fiolinenes morgenlys
vakler jeg inn i en ny dag
enda en gang, og du tar smilende imot
med nykokt egg or ristet loff
spør om jeg har sovet godt

DNA-molekylet og himmelrommet
suser som vind i min hjerne
når jeg rører melken ut i kaffen
at ja takk
jeg har sovet godt

Dag Sundby

54

SLEEPLESS

Yes indeed I'm deathly
afraid of heaven's heights
and the brown spots on my hands
The nightly concerts
of heartbeat and kettledrums
tuba and percussion
Allegro con fuoco
in steadily narrowing spirals
toward infarction's inevitable climax

Rescued by violins of morning light
I stagger into a new day
once more, and you meet me
smiling with fresh-boiled egg and toast
ask whether I slept well

DNA-molecules and outer space
hiss like wind in my brain
as I stir milk into the coffee
Why yes thanks
I slept well

J.K.

PERLE DER INNE

Min elskede
kan jeg ikke se
men en korona stråler ut fra ham
derfor venter jeg på natten

Stjernehopene i hans øyne
tennes i mine
vi leker i pleiaders lys

Min elskedes hender er
to østersskall
tett sluttet
jeg vil dykke i dypet
legge sjelens øre inntil:
hva gror i dem —
perle derinne
er du sort eller hvit?

I underets time
åpner seg hans hender
morgenen møter meg

Anbjørg Pauline Oldervik

PEARL IN THERE

I cannot see
my beloved
but a corona radiates from him
so I wait through the night

Starclusters in his eyes
are kindled in mine
we play in the Pleiades' light

My beloved's hands are
two oyster shells
tightly closed
I will dive to the depths
lay my soul's ear upon them:
what grows in them —
pearl in there
are you black or white?

In the hour of wonder
his hands open
morning meets me

J.K.

MOT ET LYS

Hva rørte lett min arm
streifet svakere enn pust
mine lukkede øyne
en usynlig
nær min munn

Hvem merker med skyggefingre
mine tinninger
dreier mitt hode
som i en magnets felt

mot et lys
innenfor lyset

Anbjørg Pauline Oldervik

TOWARD A LIGHT

What barely touched my arm
brushed more faintly than breath
my closed eyes
the unseeable
near my mouth

Whose shadowfingers trace
my temples
turn my head
as in a magnet's field

toward a light
within the light

J.K.

IV   *cobalt shadows*

ELEGY FOR ELDERBERRY AUNTS

At the edge of once upon a time
two fragile pastel figures bend,
prod for berries
with toe, crutch, branch.
Forays into underbrush
and tangled memory
yield little fruit.
The air is still
still enough
(hold off, summer's end…)
to let blend
the lay of pine in wind
with shush of willow,
merging the now,
then, and then again
of widows
as recall and reunion
dissolve.
Out of tune by half a tone
with each other's refrain
two mourning doves
remember summer.

KATHY FISKUS

Today, after fifty-three years,
your name came back to me
for the first time.
You and I were both six
when a radio told
of your fall
down a very deep well.
For days they tried to reach you,
pull you out alive.
They spoke to you
through a loudspeaker.
Somehow they could tell
that you were conscious.
I disappeared for hours
sliding myself into the crawl space
behind our scratchy brown sofa
under the east window
that faced Ohio, where you were —
kneeling back there
to look outside
at gathering clouds,
will your rescue,
imagine who you were,
to wonder if you
could look up the tunnel
and see sky. Newscasts
brought word of you
until the rescue failed.
I grieved alone,
told no one.
Today

your name suddenly sprang
to mind. If one
can write to the past,
Kathy Fiskus,
let these lines fall
as gently over you
as snow and remembrance.

FEVER

I dream there is no more bread.
The Eucharist is consecrated
of the only white thing remaining:
string. I swallow it.
The mattress draws me in
like quicksand. Overnight
my body takes root
in the bedclothes.
They make heavy my rising.

MISANTROPISK

Lite gjør meg tristere enn lystighet
Latterens støyende sekunder
Champagnens glitter
Guirlandernes renneløkker
Nyttårsaftenens autodaféer

Alle disse bajasserier
Middelmådige illusjoner og
Hvem ler høyest
Hvem ler lengst
I hvor mange sekunder kan du le
Menneske før du eksploderer
Som en mislykket nyttårsrakett og
Faller fresende til jorden

Dag Sundby

MISANTHROPIC

Few things make me sadder than hilarity
Deafening seconds of laughter
Glittering champagne
Garlands coiled like nooses
New Year's death decrees

All this buffoonery
Mediocrity's illusions and
Who laughs loudest
Who laughs longest
How many seconds can you laugh
Mankind before you explode
Like a fireworks disaster and
Plunge sizzling into the ground

J.K.

SOLEFALL

Lyset lister seg
Som Gud i den brennende busk
Inn i krattskogen blir
Hengende fast der inne og sliter
Seg til blods på lange torner
Siver ut på andre siden og farger
Himmelen dryppende rød
Før den synker i havet
For å lindre sine sår

Dag Sundby

SUNSET

The light seeps
Like God into the burning bush
Gets caught fast
In the thicket and struggles
Itself bloody on long thorns
Trickles out the other side and colors
The sky dripping red
Before sinking into the sea
To soothe its wounds

J.K.

REQUIEM FOR RICHARD GILMAN

(Jan. 31, 1944 - Nov. 11, 2002)

"I'll be back in time for Thanksgiving."
Indeed, you are. It has stopped snowing on this day before
    the holiday.
The sun is a bare bulb dimmed by rushing clouds.
Curtains of powdery snow fall from evergreen branches
at the whim of a cemetery wind.

As though from a great distance,
a voice has read psalm and prayer over you.
Two old men, the last mourners to leave,
speak of weather and the miniscus. As their voices recede,
your great silence begins.

At your graveside, a white birch watches over
flowers and footprints of your beloved ones who stood
before the coffin engulfed in wordless
grief, outrage, uncomprehending loss, your murderer
    having taken
two weeks to return from Zimbabwe what was your strong
    body.

It is a monstrosity of days, a calamity of dawns and dusks
that you do not live, Richard Gilman. You defied a tyrant
and were martyred trying to feed and educate children
he was starving: the generation
whose parents did not vote for him.

I wait until gravediggers pause in their task,
then cast three handfuls of earth over you —
and so, farewell to the hero I met only four times.
"Here, clean your hands on my jacket."
A workman's kindness rekindles life.

SILENCE

After clouds have emptied and cleared
cobalt shadows of evergreen
may lengthen across trackless white
in the still churchyard.

THE SPIRAL ELEVATOR SHAFT

In a dream
I push the UP button
and step inside.
The door closes
and the cage tilts
rising and spinning —
invention
of a mad architect.
Disoriented
without daylight or horizon
desperate for balance
inside a tornado tipping
I fight the eerie slant and whirl
of ascent
struggle too hard
to notice we've stopped.

A door slides open. Light
crosses a threshold:
a cappella colors
mural of music
fluency in motion
tide of incoming words.
I need not have flailed
all the way up —
enough just to lean
let spin
and be carried.

IN JANUARY

In January
    each day has two dawns —
    the grey one, when first praises
    rise from chill monastery chapels
    and the one which rims
    early pastels in gold.

I wake for both
    with warm black fur pressed
    to the shape of my waist,
    a paw crossing my wrist.
    Passing bootsteps crunch and squeak,
    snowfall muffles traffic sounds.

In January
    magic colors have left the trees:
    holiday ornaments,
    October leaves,
    summer birds — gone.
    Branches are stripped to the poem.

In January
    north sky turns itself
    inside out
    looking for light to shed
    but all it holds in store
    is more snow.

At this moment of the year
    roles are exchanged:
    sky bends down
    to borrow light
    cast upward by snowfields
    into the darkness.

In deep winter nights
    amber tea steams in clear glass
    and words remain
    more important than sleep.
    Snow is my Godmother,
    Blizzard my Muse.

O MOST MYSTERIOUS

O most mysterious Spring
when sunset paints onion domes
above urban brickyard
seen from my balcony,
when traffic and sirens dissolve
as Rachmaninov's *All-Night Vigil*
announces Holy Week
in the world...
O mysterious pause
when Nature holds her breath:
snow melts, ice thaws
but no tree is ready
to burst into pale green...

A full moon rises
teased by pale fog
now into a comet shape,
now into a giant quarter note
from some vast musical score.
Those who spend this night in dim cafés
forming the new century's poetry,
those approaching Passover
or on their knees
in Passiontide ritual — all remember
who was here last year, who is lost
to slaughter and suicide bombings,
while war and pollution
violate the planet

that gives us
so gently
once again
another
Spring.

FLEETING JEWEL

In Memoriam: Denise Levertov

*"Last night the planet Venus made its closest approach
to Earth in many years. Earthshine on the dark portion
of the moon made visible many details of its contours."*

(News broadcast, April 20, 1988)

You opened a microcosm
in an hour's poetry reading
and became the focus
of concentric
English Department circles.
You knew my thanks:
our eyes had met during applause.
No need therefore
for me to stand in line
to speak to you.
Outside,
a slender silver moon-curve,
elegant ear,
had lured a planet
close as an earring —
coveted, perfect jewel
borrowed for a night or two.
I ran back
into the hot auditorium.
"There's a poem
hanging in the sky!"
You heard,
and came to see.
Side by side,
rapt at the brilliance,
we watched
until the view was clouded
by voices calling your name.

LOUISE AND THE STAR SHOWER

"Often a star was waiting for you to notice it."
— *Rainer Maria Rilke*

Your arrival in the pasture at 2:00 a.m.
is heralded by one astonished Schnauzer
dashing ahead as chief usher.
Concert hall, art gallery and ballet
awaited your arrival in vain
on this August night.
Stately at any hour, you take a seat
as joyous barks prelude
the one event
where earthlings are incidental
and the performance opens
with or without us.
Meteors charge past, stars break rank on impulse,
the heavens are at play — exempt
from their staid patterns. A whimsical God rummages
in His toybox, undisturbed by lack of privacy,
no doubt casting a conspiratorial wink
in your direction... For you, who disdain
organized worship, have remained guest of honor
throughout this four-hour Gala. With dawn as finale,
you uncork a coffee thermos, forgotten all night,
after which heading home for breakfast
becomes your way back from awe
to wide wondrous earth's
everyday...

AFTER THE PICNIC

Boy child
asleep on moss:
dreams gather round
your supine grace
each eager to own
your afternoon
The brook laps enough
to keep silence
from waking you
Leaves cast
a dappled spell
lending transparency
to your slenderness
With trust for a garment
you let repose
lavish itself
upon you

BREAKAWAY II

Thirty-five summers, no, thirty-six
and none so cold as this —
the summer of my escape
So much can come away with one
whose heart is the traveling case
Like Christina of Sweden
berobed and running
I want to flee down stairs
course through cloisterways
find the gate unguarded
cross a wide lawn
disappear among trees
reach a meeting point
and with pounding heart
await rescue

I have not walked a beach
heard a siren
decided for myself
owned anything
for half a lifetime

Pre-dawn stillness passes
into morning ritual —
chant of Lauds
strong convent coffee
procession to Mass
the last breakfast
chant of Terce
I give an elderly nun
her wheelchair outing
leave workspace pristine

prepare to forsake
all but my vows:
community life
Abbey enclosure
my sisters
chant of the ages

The worm that has entered here
fattens on poverty
laughs at chastity
craves obedience
oozes truth-strangling
tentacles

I slip away at Vespers
but remember the bells
re-enter
climb up
grasp the ropes

You my sisters
clad in holy garb of my stitching —
I ring you to prayer
ring you my farewell

Truth comes out
like a bell ringing
in the tower of the throat

PSALM FOR A NEW MILLENNIUM

Morning You permeate the dawn,
      Your stillness liquifies my bones.
      There is nothing left in me
      but surrender.
      I ride the prayer of day's opening
      wherever it leads,
      even if to the abyss:
      I could let go of breathing
      to plunge forever into You,
      but You exhale once again
      and my lungs fill with life.

Noon   At the moment
      You lift me to Yourself
      have we surged further
      into eternity
      than human mind can fathom?
      Do You not place Yourself
      as close to me at this instant
      as promised for a future
      beyond time? Yet I know You more
      by the longing You rouse in me
      than by the clarity I desire of You.

Evening You, my safe passage,
      have brought me once again
      to You — each night's shelter
      where I am held in secret.

V   high clear notes

KOSCHKA

Odd that, in all the years we've known each other,
my cat and I, until tonight,
have never before met on the street
(she with her friend, I with mine).
An exchanged glance determines
there's to be no purring,
no ankle-rubbing, no stooping
to stroke bewhiskered cheek and flickered ear —
nor other such loss of dignity —
just
one glance:
enough for recognition,
greeting (when on a public thoroughfare)
and a comrades' agreement
to maintain the restraint our pride imposes.

HAIKU

I

Just-hatched reptile turns
Green in gravel, gray in grass:
New to lizardry.

II

Longlegged spiders
Loving in the shade: problem
Is — Whose feet are whose?

III

Madcap zigzaggers
tailgate at top speed: squirrel
chase through silken grass.

CENTIPEDE

Out the window you go,
rescued once
from a bathtub deluge
and twice from becoming
a cat's appetizer.
While airborne,
do all your fourteen pairs of legs
swim in space?
Now you will have made
a soft landing
on something green —
neither drowned nor eaten alive.
How does an arthropod
react to a near-death experience?
Me, I'd check my whole long torso
expecting feathers
after this apparent rebirth.
I'd lift every limb in turn
to see if a set of wings
might be sprouting somewhere.
Would an appetite shift
now send me in search of
earthworms?
If not,
would life be humdrum again
after five minutes
back at sub-grass level,
just as before that long climb
up the drainpipe? And
would I still have dreams
of being able to fly?

MOCKINGBIRD THE RAPPER

Each verse to be read aloud at top speed
without taking a second breath

It's nifty it's nifty it's nifty
boy oboy oboy oboy
to sit sit sit prettily prettily
sit sit prettily
Chipper and perky chipper and perky
chipper chipper chipper and perky perky perky
Effusive and talkat–effusive and talkative
Theory dearie theory dearie
Spidery pillow spidery pillow
spidery spidery spidery sip sip sip
Petrified pottery petrified petrified pottery

Utter veracity utter utter veracity Felicity
Tipsy and tottery tipsy and tottery
Robbery brigade brigade brigade
robbery Give it give it give it back
Hyper gregarious hyper gregarious
hyper-hyper-hyper Hyper gregarious
Punch in the bowl punch in the bowl
punch punch punch Bring in the bunch
Bring it bring it bring it

Choose it and chew it Choose it and chew it
Pottery pottery pottery Chow chow chow
Choose it and chew it
Berry berry berry Shoe shoe shoe
Precious dilemma precious dilemma
precious precious precious
dilemma dilemma dilemma Help help help

Manikin there Manikin there
manikin manikin manikin
Out of sight out of sight out of sight
fly fly fly
Really remember me really remember me
really really really fly fly fly
Out of sight out of sight
fly fly 'Bye

DINNER IS POSTPONED

Two little bodies lie still,
caught in stove wiring.
The repairman backs off, muttering
"I don't do snakes."
It is my sister,
rubber-gloved,
who reaches in
and sees, and knows
"The snake died hungry,
but the mouse died free."

OPEN 24 HOURS

Heyado'in?

Hey.

Bad scene?

Yup.

Waddeedo? Shood umseff?

Wan't no way'a holdnum back.

Soosahd? Didee turn'd on you?

Naw. Jes' shod umseff.

Y'wannah chock-covuhd doughnut?

Yep. Coffee black.

"FREAKING AWESOME!"

From the Vermont village funeral home
come high volume sounds of rock band practice.
"Freaking awesome!" yells a passerby
toward the open window.
The mortician's son and friends, hot at it,
might make the dead wonder if it's time yet...

LAST OF SUMMER

Where do they go —
our Funeral Home's Finest —
when unneeded for an hour
during Mass and Eulogy?
Whitest shirts, blackest vests
lend formality
to the Heart of Torrington Cafe.
A brief hush falls
over the Saturday regulars —
java sippers in shorts and
sweatshirts.
Perhaps they wonder
if these are mourners
here to brace up on caffeine
— or perhaps the diminuendo
admits a whispered semi-prayer:
not my time yet
not in my circle
no, not for a long time
not me
not yet

OFFSTAGE CHOREOGRAPHY

Feet first, she leans
out the Chevy door
(one arm missing,
one withered)
and faces him
with neck and jaw set
for the grip of his hands
around her head.
Locked in motion
they take the outward swing
in perfect rhythm
and he's got her
clean on her feet,
another week's shopping trip
complete.

LIMERICK

for Emily Patterson, a Nutmeg Conservatory
graduate, now a member of the Joffrey Ballet

E. Patterson, creature ethereal
Is dancing with style imperial.
  Her elegant grace
  And her fleetness in space
Make *my* movements all seem rhinocerial.

MANHATTAN STREET MUSIC

I

Passersby ignore
the crescendo of meows.
Frantic, the little man fumbles
with a cane in rusty grating.
Fooled, I stop to ask,
"Trapped cat?"
He straightens up
and bows, pleased.
"Just an imitation."
Relieved, I walk on.
All that meowing
has warmed him up.
On the street behind me
an aria begins.

II

Bulky overcoat,
slow scrape trudge drag
of heavy heels along cement:
someone alone on Christmas Day.
I greet him in passing.
Caught short,
not expecting a merry
anything,
he frowns.
Moments later
his response

catches up with me
down the block:
two high clear notes,
whistled.

MOZART

Med blekkflekkede fingre
midt mellom et gjesp og en latter
skrev du din store finale
— Send hit punsjen
— kle av piken
— begrav min mor

Som stenstøttens grep
om Don Giovannis hånd
skrev du din dødssang
med påholden penn
natt etter natt
— Send hit punsjen
— drep kreditorene
Det er nå jeg er
Nå
Requiem

Dag Sundby

MOZART

With ink-spattered fingers
between yawning and laughing
you wrote your great finale
— Send in the punch
— undress the wench
— bury my mother

Like the stone statue's grip
on Don Giovanni's hand
you wrote your deathsong
with pen clenched
night after night
— Send in the punch
— kill the creditors
It is now I exist
Now
Requiem

J.K.

ANDRÉS SEGOVIA

(1893 - 1987)

Yesterday a silence fell
in Spain.
How shall the guitar
retrieve its voice
without you
who once said to a youth,
"Have the grace to stop talking
so I can begin to know you"?

IN CONCERT

for Marina Porchkhidze and Vladimir Shinov

Grand piano, four hands:
jubilation
caprice
romance
lament
from every age of mankind
rise in sound waves
over New England.

Longing that began
in the first human heart
cries out here.

Grief that filled the first eyes
is wept by this piano.

As truth becomes song
the cosmos bends to listen
to the hands that reveal it.

ODE TO CHOCOLATE

for Charlotte Story and with a deep bow to Lisel Mueller,
whose poem "Not Only the Eskimos" inspired this

Present at summit conferences and in the nursery
it has the power to test strength of character,
break concentration, heal the day's woes,
affect one's style and appearance.
It has caused career changes!
Though a whisper of its name quickens heartbeats,
let us strive to remain calm while recalling

the grainy chocolate on a furtive finger
withdrawn from the mixing bowl,
thick chocolate in factory melting vats,
Red Alert chocolate, that attacks
under cover of darkness
and changes hip measurements by morning;
white chocolate, that wolf in sheep's clothing;
the surreal chocolate Dali did not intend us to see
in his dripping paintings;
chocolate glue that holds witch-built
gingerbread houses together in forests;
the chocolate stage designers hide
in Nutcracker scenery, Act II.

Disastrous chocolates:
blonde, giftwrapped seashellshapes
that had to be twice bought in Rotterdam,
the first batch having been sampled into oblivion;
that chocolate chess set won at the expense
of a diet, after innocent purchase
of Little League raffle tickets;

chocolate intemperance that is, if not blessed,
at least condoned because it goes
to support the local ballet school…
photos of chocolate cut from magazines
to grace the dolls' tea table;
Russian chocolate and vodka remembered
from a New Year's Eve at the Bolshoi;
a classic of feline fur, as in
Chocolate Point Siamese;
the hot chocolate that goes with snow clouds
whether or not you ski;
the dark, the bitter, the milk —
whose inner secrets of cherry or coconut
are compared yet again
by earnest ladies
on overstuffed sofas;
chocolate chips, close to melting through
their cookie dough…

Whipped cocoa, syrup, frosting, truffles, mousse,
hot fudge, flaming liqueur:
a total condemnation of carob
as countless petite silhouettes
are abandoned forever
due to that first
small, fragrant
foil-wrapped
slender-tipped
ruinous
Chocolate
Kiss.

FOR THE CHILDREN OF ZIMBABWE

written with Lisa Bosworth

How would it be to hang upon a clothesline?
Stretched out so far,
I'd wonder: Are
those distant dangling toes mine?

I'd swing all morning long in our back garden.
Sunbeams would race
through leafy lace:
green light to wrap our yard in.

With billowed sleeves and puffed-out shirts beside me,
by shoulders pinned
I'd let the wind
blow playful gusts that dried me

'til Mother came to take me down and fold me.
I'd wait for lunch
then eat so much
that clothespins couldn't hold me!

CONNECTION DELAYED

Marble-eyed waitresses
bring warm cottage cheese
and cool chowder.
Bookshop offers
Today's Woman Fulfilled and
*How to Put the Need
Back in Needlepoint.*

Five hours in a small airport.
How could I have forgotten
to bring poetry?

VI   *magnetic north*

WHITE ON WHITE

Blizzard whitens
against an airport window.
While I keep watch
the scene shifts:
an Oriental mural
spreads across the wide pane.
In remote winter mountains
a hermit's hut perches on craggy heights
among snow-clad evergreens.
Far below, a pavilion
with upturned roof edges
begins to catch white flakes
falling beside a frozen lake.
I lean forward, absorbed in the view.
Are those three travelers on foot
bound for the country inn
just around the bend?
Suddenly my forehead bumps
the freezing pane. Gone in an instant,
hut, trees and pavilion
prove to be flaws in plate glass.
Wind gusts outside part the whiteness
to reveal slow-motion courtesies
among jets towed backward,
meal service carts and baggage ferries...

Enough airport lounge Limbo —
Let me jump into a snowdrift
or onto a jet rising
toward the North.

MAGNETIC NORTH

Somewhere a magnet
pulls my blood.
The soul in my blood leans north.
I set out by train
from Oslo to Nidaros:
cathedral, riverside lamps,
faces memorized by candlelight
in a cellar café.
A second train crosses
the Arctic Circle overnight.
Through closed eyelids
a flare of crimson
awakens me —
Dawn has put a torch
to mountain snows.
At Bodø
all trees and train tracks end.
Onward into the Far North
we glide by ferry, docking
six hours later among
Lofoten herring boats.
What is a choreographer
doing here? In fact
I am almost home.

Seared by February's Polar wind
I take refuge in a new building
with public space for rent.
Wide windows face a silent choir
of white-robed mountain peaks.
In my solitude
opposite theirs
prepared for communion,
I dance.

INTO THE SAGA

The mountain must have trembled at such a fall.
The Elg (lord of the forest,
Norwegian brother to elk and moose)
lies surrounded by faces ruddy in torchlight
under hunters' caps of riotous color.
Invited to sit on the animal's shoulder
I feel tremendous muscle mass
slack under his pelt.
At once we lift off, I and the soul of the Elg
above tips of fir trees pointing up
beyond mountain crest: night sky opens wide,
past blends with present, saga with reality.
There to the south, the Hall of the Mountain King
lures Per Gynt to new revels
while beside a distant lake
his mother Aase wrings her poor hands.
Epochs parade past: Viking,
troll, reindeer, pilgrim king,
villain, priest, bard and princess.
Gudrid's journey begins anew,
Kristin Lavransdatter reaches Nidaros Cathedral,
Saint Olav blesses the throngs,
a queen seems to be running away.
From antiquity all of them know the Elg and his kind.
Overhead, shifting pillars of light
color the firmament, swoop
and plunge around us
as Aurora Borealis receives the soul of the Elg.
I cling to his pelt while the hues shimmer and shift
then slow (dreamlike) down
bringing back into focus the bright caps,
the laughing faces around me,

elated at having a foreigner see their triumph.
It has taken this prime team of hunters
eight days to drive the Elg from forest to field
and a split second for a proud marksman
to burst the heart. Though a tractor will draw him
down the mountainside to become
food and warmth for villagers below,
the Elg and I keep our secret:
no one guesses how far we have come
in a moment's travel, moving not an inch
from where he lies on his right side,
eye to eye now with the Polar stars.

BY NORTHERN LIGHT

I   Lofoten Winter

Mountains like giant wolf teeth
rim treeless Lofoten dawn.
Sunrise and sunset
share the same hour.
Tang of herring
whets the sting of Arctic air.
An artist paints
sleeping women who dream of fish
and fish that dream of women.
Outside, a sudden snow
bites and blinds.
Folk on foot
lean hard
into booming wind.

II   Stormwatch

Eyes that once were blue
turn again to face the coming snows.
Paler now, they've lost a dash of color
with each winter's wind.

III   The Moss Gatherer

By fingertip, by centimeter,
he knows the mountainside.
His knees are damp with its earth.

A jacket the color of lichen
curves to his back.
Huge hands probe for wild moss,
piling bundle and clump
into wooden crates
that will carry this harvest
unbruised
to florists half a world away.
Secrets the mountain tells
make his eyes dance
under the worn visor.
When at last he gets to his feet
a burst of slanted light
parts high clouds.

IN MOSCOW

At Novodevichy Convent
it is twenty-six below —
indoors. Cold gnaws
through boots into marrow.
People stamp and pace
to endure it.
In sanctuary darkness
candelabras flare, haloed faces
gleam their benediction
from a high iconostasis.
The single window in a passageway
will remain frosted over for months.
I rub hard and blow on it
until a fingertip-sized circlet
is thawed — enough to peer outside
onto snow-crusted paths
and domes over pastel towers.
"New Maidens' Convent":
how many young widows
have stood at this window
with hearts and hopes
forever icebound —
here, where I am standing
at this most frozen moment
of my life?

ST. PETERSBURG: THE MARIINSKY

Not as a stranger —
more as a homing pigeon
after thirty-four years —
straight from hotel check-in
on feet that simply know the way
I return to the Mariinsky Theatre.

Her venerable and gleaming majesty
poised beside Kryukov Canal
in a fresh coat
of intense Key Lime green
with whipped cream trim
is like a lady of rank and dignity
during a solemn public event
whose eyes suddenly twinkle
as she yields to a daydream of desserts.

Displayed in a quiet corner of the foyer
apart from glossy ad banners
one large poster hand-lettered in Cyrillic
— like a greeting from a past still alive —
announces upcoming performances.
Among great opera houses
in a world of computer graphics
a single anonymous calligrapher
shows us how it was
once upon Petrouchka's time.

MAY NIGHT

On Anniversary Weekend —
Peter's three hundred and first —
citizens pour into parks and squares.
The Orthodox Liturgy of Pentecost Vigil
has just resounded in St. Isaac's
with enough power
to dissolve sin and doubt
so long as its *a cappella* tones
hang in the air.
On this night that will barely darken
revelers fill Admiralty Park
wearing elephant ears,
rubber antlers,
cheekbones enhanced with hot pink foam,
masks with purple eyebrows.
Even the linden trees join Carnival mode,
arching over park paths
in full foliage finery.
No one sits on park bench seats —
perched on the backrests
they smoke, tell secrets,
lead up to a kiss,
imagine or relive certain conquests.
Sweet drink stands and sausage vendors
keep a respectful distrance
from The Bronze Horseman.
Forever poised to charge,
perhaps he too relives conquests
while before him a sassy trombone
slides a note of sarcasm into "God Bless America."
The young surge into Palace Square,

willingly pack themselves
shoulder to throat
to await a rock concert.
Cellist Knyasev is at Philharmonic Hall,
Temirkanov conducts Elgar and Berlioz.
The Mariinsky Opera is sold out.
The satisfied spill out of restaurants,
while even the café cat on Malaya Morskaya
thrives on scraps, and the affection
of strangers.

City of Peter,
how many of your children
never saw such bounty?
Though we may not spare them much thought
the nameless ones are also here —
those who died while forced to build this city.
Everywhere we tread on their bones.
Don't we see movement in the breeze?
Perhaps their fluttering souls return
at the moment of celebration...

ENCOUNTER

Moonrise
from Vasilievsky Island —
immense twin pearls
luminous, faintly pink:
one ascends in languor
over spire and dome
of St. Petersburg skyline,
the other, buoyant,
bobs across the Neva toward me.
Under the spell of splendor —
and perhaps a little after-hours refreshment —
another moongazer
dressed for the office
wavers, walks on, no,
weaves,
smacks into my left side
and finds support against a wrought-iron fence.
She speaks torrents of Russian,
wants a light,
gestures toward the moon.
Why not be agreeable?
"Da!" I respond
and we remain there
transfixed in the white night.
"Eedou," I say at last —
"I'm going" — and
"Eedou!" she repeats,
grabbing my elbow.
What is all this she tells me
as we turn
toward Lt. Schmidt Bridge?

At the Arts Academy
almost as though expected
a third woman joins us.
We mount the bridge
into time out of time,
try several languages,
not finding a common tongue
pause halfway across the great river,
suspend all disbelief,
are fervent friends
with one moon high above us
and one below.

To walk in the City of Peter
past midnight along the canals
is to understand each other
perfectly.

BENJAMIN AND ANNA

He has the offhand look of a novelist
about to stun the world
with his latest. She —
with powerful arms and level gaze —
could be a sculptress.
Seated side by side in a glass café
the two speak Flemish,
their elegant profiles
turned toward each other.
If I could commission
a master painter, their portrait
would soon hang on a museum wall.
In English, I tell them so
and, amid their laughter
at such an idea,
am invited to their table.
Homeward-bound to Belgium
they have spent forty years
in African agriculture.
A reckless friendship begins
though we are unlikely to meet
a second time on earth.
"You have a mission in life,"
Benjamin tells me before we part,
"Let's hope they listen to you."

Outside, shielding their eyes
from the sun, they turn, wave,
and rejoin the throng
along Nevsky Prospekt.

PETERSBURG PILGRIMAGE

Following
in holy footsteps
along vast avenues
over bridges of legend
I roam streets and squares,
trace three canals
mile after mile,
walk the distance
to island's end, where
at Alexander Nevsky Monastery
Russia's revered artists
rest in Tikhin Cemetery.
Alone in light rain
I find their graves,
bring flowers
to Tschaikovsky, Petipa,
Balakirev, Dostoevsky.
Clouds thicken, it pours.
To Rimsky-Korsakov, Glinka,
Mussorgsky, many more
somewhere close by
go all the other bouquets
tossed high
— a shower of petals
to fall with drenching rain —
in homage from one
who is still above ground.

SIDEWALK SAINTS

I   St. Petersburg, 2004

One kneels all day on cement
near Kazan Cathedral,
a worn plastic bag
covering her outstretched palm.
Those who pause before her
must bow in order to give.
Nearby stands another
holding an empty cup.
Their right hands move
in ceaseless *molto adagio*
signing the Cross again and again
to ask and to thank:
their work on earth.

II   New York City, 2005

At Madison Square Park
she holds out both palms, empty.
Huge dark eyes gaze upward
with wisdom and dignity
that burn into me.
To hand her something
is both privilege and blessing.
Black babushka and silver hair
are her only crown
yet a trace of her royalty
will live in me
so long as memory carries her.

III   Oslo, 2006

A year later
glancing up from a poem
in a café opposite the National Theater
I spot their sister crossing toward me
dressed in black, with light all around her.
As she passes the window, I drop everything
and dash out for her blessing.
In Russian
she lifts her "Thanks to God!"
We stand eye to eye
for a moment's handclasp.

Who knows what would become of us all,
St. Petersburg, Manhattan, Oslo or the world
without these ladies in black
and their plea for our cities,
for whatever compassion
lives in us?

BETWEEN REHEARSALS

I

Walking through Oslo
I watch my shadow
— cast by night sun —
hurry along a stone wall.
Even that shadow
has changed
in ten days abroad.

II

Among sculptures
beside the ballet studio:
a lifesize reindeer.
Every day
young riders cling
to his antlers.
Though parents wave
nearby
the outward journey
has begun.

III

In the pew beside me
at Sankt Dominikus
the young man grabs my hand
with a wide smile

but cannot speak. After Mass
while others remain
bowed in prayer
he nudges me expectantly,
begins humming on true pitch
the River Kwai film theme.
Another nudge, and I give in —
our soft duet becomes
communion.

IV

On the last night
one by one
departing cars start
downhill.
The dancers are leaving.
Now they look up and wave,
now their faces float away.
I lean toward them
from a studio window.
The fjord grows misty.
Hanging birch
and undulating lilacs
shimmer, waving
green and lavender veils
— farewell, farewell —
all through
the pearl-bright night.

V

How to translate
"Hjertespor"
for an English art catalog?
At first, clumsy mouthfuls
of word failure.
Perhaps no other language
should dare describe
the mystery
of leaving behind forever
a part of oneself
in the far North:
"There where the heart
has been..."

HOMECOMING

I

Sunset at 36,000 feet over Newfoundland

If the blood contains the soul
whose soul is it
curved around earth's rim
as though to embrace
an entire planet?

II

From a street kiosk in St. Petersburg
or an open-backed truck in New Haven
one can buy fresh roses
past midnight.

SOLI DEO GLORIA

NOTES

Page 53, "*Sub Specie Aeternitatis*": "From the Viewpoint of Eternity."

Page 69, "Requiem for Richard Gilman." Dick Gilman was a computer professional who loved adventurous traveling in natural areas and distant places. He began bringing educational materials and food supplies to disadvantaged and starving children at a rural school in Zimbabwe. On his third trip there, he passed through a checkpoint and was asked to return again with a particular document. He did so, voluntarily, and was shot as he began to drive away from the checkpoint.

Page 78, "Breakaway II." A friend of mine was a cloistered nun for many years. When influences that threatened her vows and her vocation reached into the cloister, it became necesssary for her to flee. "Breakway II" is partly factual, partly imaginative — an attempt to visualize that drama.

Page 102, "For the Children of Zimbabwe." Dick Gilman took this poem to Vumbunu Primary School in Watsomba, Zimbabwe, where it was used to help young children learn English. The only collaboratively-written poem in this collection, it came on a day spent with my sister Lisa Bosworth.

Page 106, "Magnetic North." The attraction held for me by all things Northern began in my youth with a film of the Bolshoi Ballet (Galina Ulanova in "Giselle," plus half a dozen "Highlights" from the repertoire). My passion for classical ballet had been nurtured only by rudimentary training, so the Bolshoi stage curtain opened an immense vista of what the ultimate dance artistry could express. Suddenly the onion domes and Russian "mythos," the sound of Russian language and music, stories by travelers there, Russian literature and poetry in translation, images of Russian forest depths, fragments of the land's history — all took over my imagination.

Early in my classical ballet career, I was able to travel to Russia with a group of teachers from London's Royal Ballet School. We were welcomed by the faculty of the school named for Agrippina Vaganova (feeder school to the Kirov Ballet in St. Petersburg) and by company teachers of the Bolshoi Ballet in Moscow. What I learned from them had a profound influence on my work, as did my ongoing study of the Russian training system. Russian Impressionist art and a return to "Mecca" have continued to magnify all that went before.

Soon after my initial trip to Russia, I was invited as guest choreographer and teacher to Oslo, Norway for the first of many artistic residencies, working with pre-professional students of the Kirkenær Ballet School, with college students (Den Norske Balletthøyskole) and later with the graduation class of the Swedish Ballet School in Stockholm. With each return engagement, new aspects of Northern culture come alive for me through contact with gifted young dancers, friendships, folklore, terrain and the captivating Norwegian language. A number of the poems and translations in this book spring from these impressions.

109

Page 197, "Into the Saga." On a holiday weekend during my first residency as guest choreographer in Norway, I was invited by friends to their mountain cabin in Rondane National Park, a six-hour drive north from Oslo. There was no running water or electricity, but firewood had been provided by neighbors. To pay them, we drove further into the mountains, and were told that an elg (a creature larger than the American elk) had been taken on the mountainside. Would we be interested in going up to see it? This was an event most Norwegians never witness, and we accepted. The elg lay on its side, with the triumphant hunters' faces torchlit around it. Partly for population control, hunting regulations are strenuous: a team of hunters must obtain a permit to take a particular gender and age, and the animal must be driven into a clearing, so as not to suffer and possibly go unfound in the forest. This skilled marksman had shot to the heart, and the animal died immediately, to provide food and warm fur clothing for villagers below. My hostess photographed the chief hunter sitting on the shoulder of the elg. As the only foreigner present, I was then honored with an invitation to sit on the elg's shoulder for another photo. Mourning the death of this magnificent animal, I sat holding its ear in one hand and touching its foreleg with the other. In the few moments of that stationary ride on the elg's shoulder, a vision of Northern folklore, fantasy, history and poetry opened for me.

Page 113, "May Night." Many who know and love the city call St. Petersburg by its founder's name: Peter.

Joan Kunsch is on the classical ballet faculty at Nutmeg Conservatory for the Arts, where she is also associate director. Guest teaching and choreography have taken her around North America and abroad, particularly to Scandinavia, England and The Netherlands. She belongs to a teaching team that has produced dancers for over fifty professional companies touring worldwide, and her choreography comprises over sixty works for concert stage, television, sacred space and outdoor sites. An artist and writer, Joan Kunsch has had work published in the U.S.A., Norway, England and India. She translates contemporary Norwegian poets, presents readings in Norwegian as well as English, and performs "Flute Meets Poem" in a duo with her sister, Kathi Byam. She lives in Torrington, Connecticut.

Dag Sundby was born in Romsdal, Norway in l934. He was educated in Classical Hebrew at the University of Oslo, and in French language and literature in Paris. He has published five novels, four collections of poetry and many short stories and articles, all of them in Bokmål, a slightly conservative form of the official Norwegian. For twenty years he lived abroad, in Paris, Prague, Brussels and Vilnius. He has now returned to live and write in his native Norway. He has received several fellowships from the Norwegian Writers' Association and the Norwegian Association of Publishers. In April of 2006, Sundby and Kunsch toured in Connecticut and New York City, giving public readings of his poems and her translations. His publications in this country include the journals *Ibis Review* (Connecticut), *Ice-Floe* (Alaska) and *Two Lines* (California).

Anbjørg Pauline Oldervik was born in 1918. Her first collection of poems, *Lytt* (*Listen*) came out in 1967. Over the years she has published eighteen books of poetry, including *Være i hemmelig ærend* (*On a Secret Errand*) and the latest in 2002, *Et hjerte vårt våpen (A Heart our Weapon)*. Anbjørg's poetry deals with the meaning of life: all her work is a great "why." Very often this cry is addressed to a Power — as a cry to God. At the same time there is a need for love and a conviction that love answers all the "why's." Anbjørg is a deeply spiritual poet, religious in the sense of searching for her roots beyond a restless world. Anbjørg is of Sami heritage, a fact she only recently discovered. This has given her a new pride and gratitude in life — for having stemmed from the Aborigines of the North. She was educated in Special Pedagogy.

COLOPHON

The typeface used in *Playing with Gravity* is ITC Galliard, which was designed by Matthew Carter in 1978. It is based on a classic font created in Antwerp during the 1560's by Robert Granjon, a French type designer who traveled widely, accepting commissions for new styles of type throughout Europe. Like the vigorous Renaissance dance after which it is named, Galliard is both formal and energetic, full of hidden surprises.

For notes, discussion questions and writing suggestions, visit
the Seminar Room of the Antrim House website:
www.AntrimHouseBooks.com/seminar.

To order additional copies
of *Playing with Gravity*
or other Antrim House titles
contact the publisher at

Antrim House
P.O. Box 111
Tariffville, CT 06081
860-217-0023
www.AntrimHouseBooks.com
AntrimHouse@comcast.net